A Kid's Life as a VIKING

by

Robin Twiddy

BEARPORT
PUBLISHING

Minneapolis, Minnesota

Credits

All images are courtesy of Shutterstock.com, unless otherwise specified. With thanks to Getty Images, Thinkstock Photo, and iStockphoto. Background texture throughout – Recurring images – YamabikaY, Tartila, TADDEUS, sumkinn, Vlada Young, Gaidamashchuk, pics five, Andrey_Kuzmin, Macrovector, Jemastock, Milano M, Oligo22, ONYXprj. Cover – Fedor Selivanov, Marti Bug Catcher, Kabardins photo. 2–3 – Gordana Adzieva. 4–5 – donatas1205, AlexAnton, New Africa, rangizzz, VaLiza. 6–7 – Alfmaler, Krakenimages.com, Lapina, Marco Ossino, Merydolla, Mind Pixell. 8–9 – 4 PM production, Everilda, Olga Kuevda, robuart, RHJPhtotos, SIRNARM USAVICH. 10–11 – BearFotos, Dmytro Buianskyi, Jaroslav Moravcik. 12–13 – Dunhill, Ievgenii Meyer, MasaMima, matryoshka, Matyas Rehak, Phakorn Kasikij, Quintanilla. 14–15 – bildfokus.se, Litvalifa, Monkey Business Images, SpicyTruffel, tan_tan, Victoria Sergeeva. 16–17 – Evil Panda (Wikimedia Commons), Hogan Imaging, matryoshka, Nomad_Soul, Paul Vinten, Valadzionak Volha. 18–19 – Captmondo (WikimediaCommons), grmarc, Macrovector, NotionPic, Olena Brodetska, Radiokafka. 20–21 – Beatrice Barberis, Creativa Images, Einsamer Schütze (Wikimedia Commons), Kateryna Onyshchuk, Oscar Peralta Anechina, Perfect_kebab. 22–23 – BNP Design Studio, Body Stock, matryoshka, GoodStudio, Red Fox studio. 24–25 – amelipulen, Anastasiia Kulikovska, Mega Pixel, Photick. 26–27 – amelipulen, ESB Professional, matryoshka, pink.mousy, Prostock-studio. 28–29 – GolF2532, gualtiero boffi, Laboo Studio, nattanan726, NotionPic, OlegDoroshin, Olga Kuevda. 30 – VaLiza.

Library of Congress Cataloging-in-Publication Data is available at www.loc.gov or upon request from the publisher.

ISBN: 979-8-88509-954-7 (hardcover)
ISBN: 979-8-88822-128-0 (paperback)
ISBN: 979-8-88822-274-4 (ebook)

For more information, write to Bearport Publishing, 5357 Penn Avenue South, Minneapolis, MN 55419.

CONTENTS

Being a KID

It's pretty tough being a kid. You have to share the TV remote. You're always being told what time to go to bed. And there is always someone in the bathroom when you need to go.

Finally, I have the control!

But how hard is it, really? If you think it is tough being a kid today, imagine what it was like living aboard a Viking ship long ago.

I'm cooler than any Viking!

There was no TV to watch, just your weird, hairy uncle singing a song about himself. You'd be so tired from rowing all day that you'd be begging for an early bed time. On top of all that, good luck finding a bathroom! That's tough!

THE VIKINGS
It's Viking time!

Get ready to go back in time and see what life was like for Viking kids.

The VIKINGS

We are from areas you now call Denmark, Norway, Sweden, Finland, and Iceland.

Before we journey through time, let's get something straight. The people we call Vikings didn't call themselves that. They were Norsemen. Only the Norse who went on **raids** were called Vikings. Also, they didn't wear horned helmets.

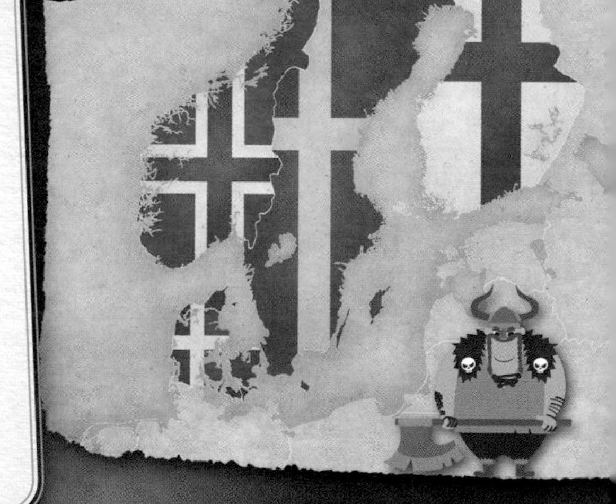

The Vikings were around more than 2,800 years ago.

Wait, my helmet isn't historically accurate?

Oh no! The Vikings have arrived!
Are you bored with farming yet?
Yeah! We should go sailing and raiding.
I like farming— I never get seasick!

Vikings were great sailors who traveled around Europe. Sometimes, they traded things with those they met. Sometimes, they attacked villages by surprise.

At home, Vikings were farmers and fishermen. These Norse men and women belonged to smaller groups called **clans**. Sometimes, clans worked together. Other times, they fought.

SURVIVING the Time

To be a Viking, you first have to survive your childhood. Want to make it to five years old? Norse children had an 8 out of 10 chance of living that long.

I will survive. And then I'm coming for you!

Today, we have doctors, hospitals, and **medicines** to help when we get sick. But Norse kids didn't. There were sometimes people in Viking villages who gave out treatments. However, they probably did it with a magical twist.

Watch me pull your kidney from this hat.

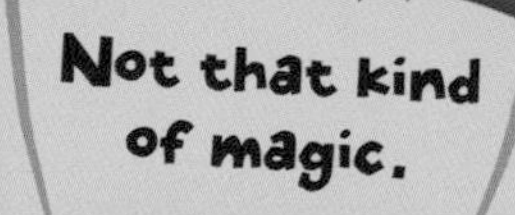
Not that kind of magic.

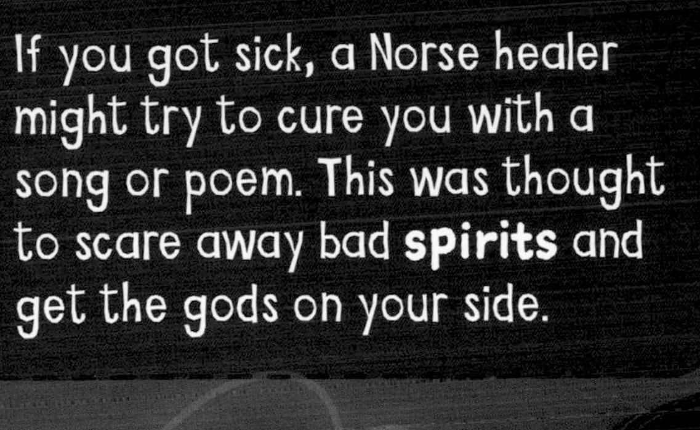

If you got sick, a Norse healer might try to cure you with a song or poem. This was thought to scare away bad **spirits** and get the gods on your side.

Roses are red, violets are blue. I have no idea how to cure you!

Vikings didn't write much, but they did carve **symbols** called runes into stone. Sometimes, runes would be used to cure people. Check your spelling, though! An old story tells of someone who used the wrong rune and made a patient even worse!

Runes

Time out! We used some **herbs**, too. It wasn't just songs and runes.

FULL House

Many **generations** of Norse men and women would often live in the same house. But you wouldn't have to share with the older generations for long. Most Vikings only lived to be about 35.

I think I look pretty good for 16!

Oh no, my dad's name is Poi!

Vikings didn't have last names. A Norse kid would take their father's name and add the Norse word for son or daughter to the end. So, if you were Erik's son, you would be Erikson.

In addition to the 10 or 20 people living in your home, you might keep pets. Vikings had pet cats, dogs, falcons, peacocks, and sometimes even bears!

When are they going to house-train Bear Bearson?

Norse kids were treated like little adults. They had to help with work around the home like everyone else. This was especially true when Dad was on a raid. He may be gone for weeks, months, or maybe forever!

Bye, Dad. Have fun on your raid.
I guess milking the cow is my job now.

HOME SMELLY Home

Great, three rooms. But there are 15 of us!

Norse homes were called longhouses. This might sound perfect for your big Viking family, but these buildings were only one room.

Sometimes, Norse families used **columns** to split the home into three parts. One was for the farm animals. Another was used as a workshop. Lastly, there was one for the family!

Baaa
GRrrrr!!!
Ow. Erik just kicked me!
What is licking my elbow?
Bjorn's feet stink!!
Mooo
Zzzzz . . .

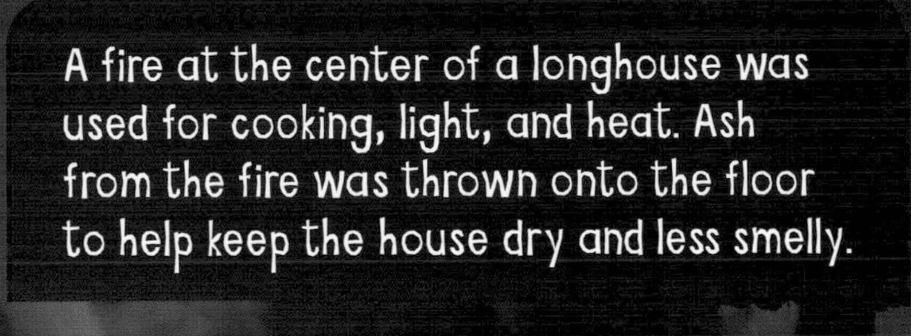

A fire at the center of a longhouse was used for cooking, light, and heat. Ash from the fire was thrown onto the floor to help keep the house dry and less smelly.

My floor isn't dirty. It's ashy!

Even with ashes on the floor, you weren't going to get away from the smell. Animals pooped and peed inside, and the Vikings probably had some serious body odor.

I never knew Vikings were so smelly!

STEW FOR ME And You

I hope you aren't a **vegetarian**. If you are, you'll have a hard time finding a meal as a kid during this time. Vikings ate a lot of meat!

It's not easy being a veggie Viking.

They ate some vegetables, but these often ended up in meat stews. Vikings would often keep adding things to the stew as the pot got low—without emptying and cleaning the pot first. So, some of those veggies may have been in the pot for weeks. *Yum!*

Can I just have a peanut butter and jelly sandwich for a change?

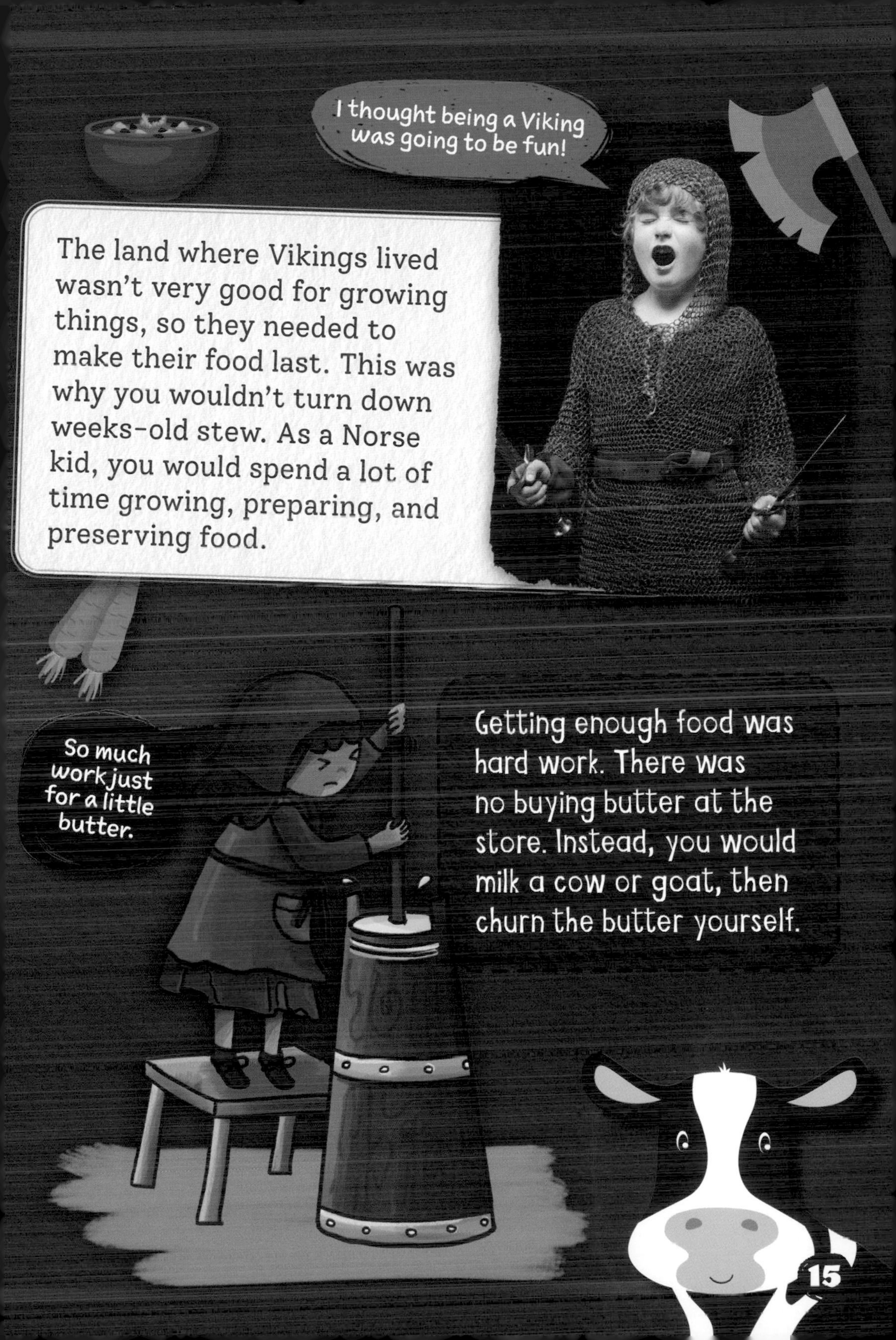
I thought being a Viking
was going to be fun!
So much
work just
for a little
butter.

The land where Vikings lived wasn't very good for growing things, so they needed to make their food last. This was why you wouldn't turn down weeks-old stew. As a Norse kid, you would spend a lot of time growing, preparing, and preserving food.

Getting enough food was hard work. There was no buying butter at the store. Instead, you would milk a cow or goat, then churn the butter yourself.

Impressing THE GODS

I'm watching you, buddy!

The Vikings had a lot of gods! Each god controlled a part of the world. They were also believed to watch over the Vikings.

Norse gods didn't care much about right and wrong. Instead, they could be won over with **sacrifices**, rune magic, and prayers.

Is this sandcastle good enough for Thor?
Silly humans. I just want to be wowed.

I love axe fighting
AND poetry.

The Vikings had long poems called the Eddas. These poems told stories about the birth of the universe, battles the Norse gods fought, and how the world would end.

Who were some of the most popular Norse gods?

Odin was the king of the gods. To gain **wisdom,** he gave away one of his eyes!

Thor was the god of thunder and strength. Warriors would **worship** him to become stronger.

Loki was the god of **mischief,** and he could not be trusted. His tricks sometimes helped the other gods, but they usually only helped Loki.

a bit
rd to

This is kind of heavy . . .

Nobody knows whose side I'm on! Heh, heh, heh . . .

Odin

Thor

Loki

In a way, the gods made the Vikings good in battle. Vikings weren't afraid to die, but they were afraid of a bad death. They believed that if you died like a hero, it would impress the gods. Then, you would be taken to Valhalla, a special afterlife for the bravest warriors.

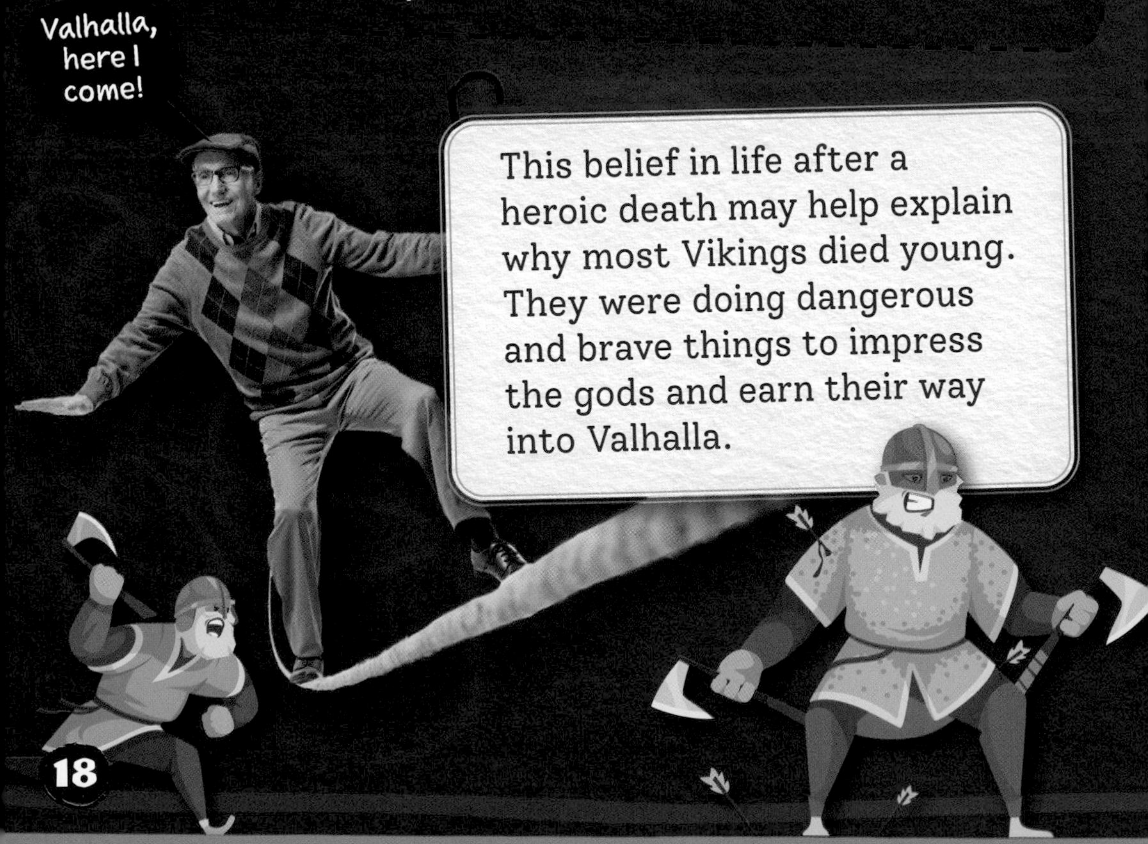
Valhalla, here I come!

This belief in life after a heroic death may help explain why most Vikings died young. They were doing dangerous and brave things to impress the gods and earn their way into Valhalla.

Sometimes, Vikings used runes and sacrifices to get the gods on their side. Don't get too attached to the sheep and goats on your farm. Before a big harvest or battle, they might have to be sacrificed!

Come on, Mr. Goat, you are off to meet Thor!

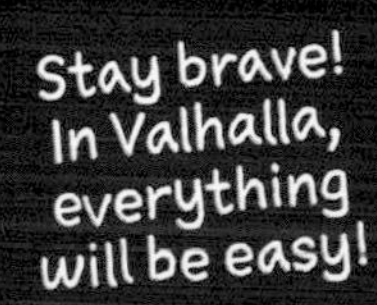

But Norse gods weren't all powerful. The Vikings believed there would be an end of the world for people and the gods. Even the gods couldn't stop this event, called Ragnarok.

It's tough being a Viking kid, Dad.

Stay brave! In Valhalla, everything will be easy!

Fierce FASHIONS

The Vikings were probably a bit smelly, but they did take a bath about once a week! They were actually very clean compared with other groups of people who lived at the same time.

Ahh, time to scrub the week's stink off.

Vikings carried around little grooming kits. Inside, there were tweezers, razors, combs, and even ear spoons! *Huh?* These small spoons were used to scoop wax out of your ears!

I wonder if they had nose spoons, too?

I hope they like my helmet. Maybe it will catch on.
My outfit is so last year.

The Vikings also cared about fashion. On the farm, men usually wore pants and long shirts. Women wore dresses. But rich Vikings wore clothes made of silk, gold, and furs gathered from far-off lands.

Do you like going to the dentist? The dentist might not be fun today, but it sure beats what Vikings did to their teeth. Some would carve lines in their front teeth. No one really knows why—maybe they thought it looked cool.

FUN and GAMES

As a Norse kid, you had to work hard, but you still got to have fun once in a while. People of all ages loved to play!

Who's the cutest kitty? Mr. Fluffyson, that's who!

Viking kids often went ice skating. Their skates were made from animal bones. They also enjoyed singing, dancing, and wrestling.

I hate wrestling. Wouldn't you rather be skating?

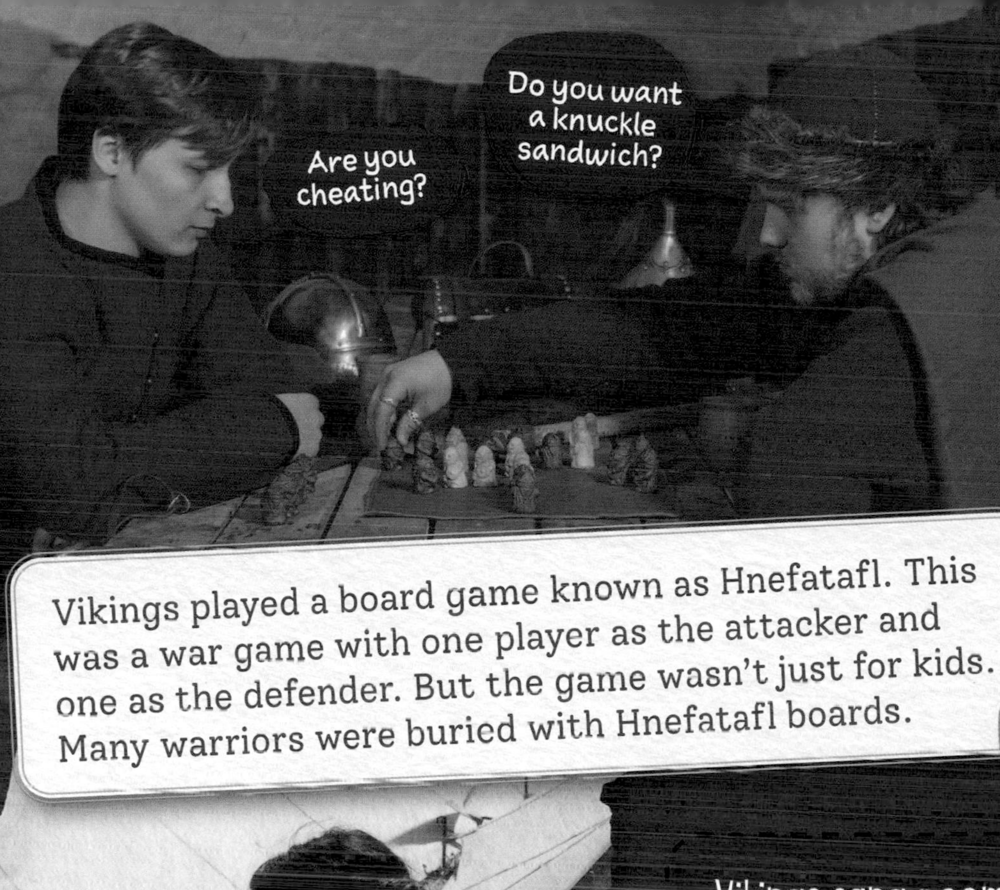
Are you cheating?
Do you want a knuckle sandwich?

Vikings played a board game known as Hnefatafl. This was a war game with one player as the attacker and one as the defender. But the game wasn't just for kids. Many warriors were buried with Hnefatafl boards.

Vikings sang poems and stories. Often, they would play along with harps, **lyres**, horns, drums, or bone whistles!

This whistle still tastes like Klara the cow.

A Norse musician and storyteller was called a skald.

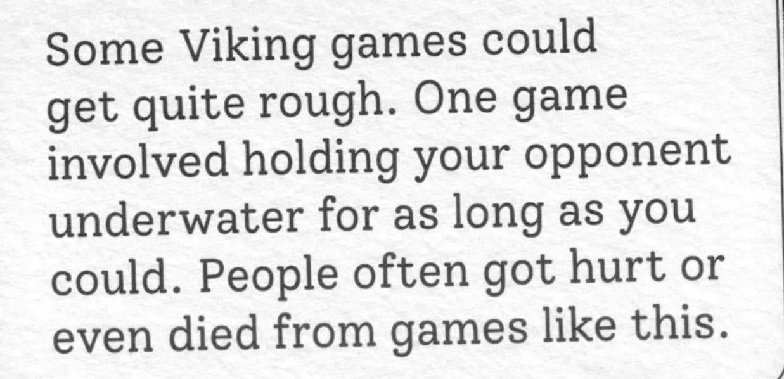

Some Viking games could get quite rough. One game involved holding your opponent underwater for as long as you could. People often got hurt or even died from games like this.

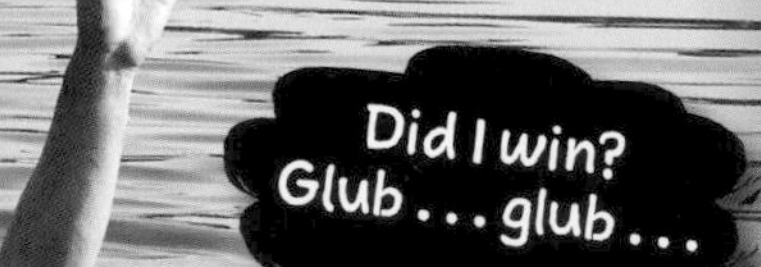
Did I win?
Glub . . . glub . . .

Vikings ran races and held weight lifting competitions. Bragging rights were serious business for the Vikings. A king might ask a Viking warrior about his **accomplishments,** and the warrior would try to impress the ruler with his sports victories.

I won this for swallowing the most water in the drowning game.
WETTEST BOY

Hey Dad! I'm just like you.
Maybe soon . . .
I should have played with more toys.

Norse toys weren't flashy or colorful like toys today. Kids played with wooden spinning tops and swords. They had bows and arrows, toy ships, and action figures. These toys were fun, but they also had a purpose.

Many toys were training tools. Playing with toy swords and warships prepared you for the real thing. Viking kids were taught how to fight! Even board games taught you how to make decisions on the battlefield!

Home SCHOOLING

You won't be learning much at Viking school—because there was no such thing! The Norse didn't have schools like we do today. But that didn't mean there was no learning.

Yay, no school! I want to be a Viking!

Most of your education would come from Mom and Dad. I hope you like spending time with your parents. Norse kids would work with, live with, and learn from their parents.

This is how to run with sharp objects in your hand.

Dad, I'm not sure you're a very good teacher.

Class, today we will learn how to make Dad a pancake breakfast.
Was it Uncle Lars who slayed a dragon? No, that was Aunt Brigitte.

Some lessons would likely be about reading and making runes. But mostly, you would learn to do what your parents did. That means cooking, sewing, farming . . . and fighting!

You would also learn poems, songs, and stories. Family history was passed down through stories told from parents to children. They weren't written down, so you'd better have a good memory.

GROWN UP

When?

Since Vikings didn't usually live very long, there wasn't much time to enjoy being a kid.

I'm no kid. I'm almost middle-aged!

Feels like yesterday I was playing with toys . . . Because it was.

Most of your childhood was spent learning skills, helping out around the house and farm, and doing chores. Then, at the young age of 16, boys would be considered men. Girls were thought of as women at 12!

As an adult, you'd likely be heading out to sea. It didn't matter if you were a boy or girl. If you were strong and could handle a sword, you would probably be joining the boat. You're going raiding!

Maybe whacking my brother with that toy sword wasn't such a good idea!

But try not to worry. From the time you were a kid, you would have been training to become a strong and skilled Viking adult.

That's TOUGH!

Do you still think being a kid today is tough? At least you don't have to deal with Norse chores, reheated stews, and smelly people all crammed into one room.

Phew!

Lucky for you, you don't need to go on raids or impress the gods. Just relax and return to your own time. And remember, it's not so bad being a kid now. It could be a lot worse!

What part of being a Viking sounds the toughest?

GLOSSARY

accomplishments difficult things that someone has done

clans groups of people related to one another or united by shared interests

columns supporting pillars or poles

generations groups of people born around the same time

herbs plants that can be used for food or medicine

lyres musical instruments with strings that are similar to harps

medicines things used or taken to fight off sicknesses or pain

mischief bad behavior that is often playful

raids sudden attacks or invasions

sacrifices gifts of value given to a god or gods in order to please them

spirits beings that are not part of this world

symbols letters, characters, or signs used in place of words

vegetarian someone who does not eat meat

wisdom good judgement and understanding

worship to show great honor or respect to

INDEX

READ MORE

Kerry, Isaac. *Science on Viking Expeditions (The Science of History).* North Mankato, MN: Capstone Press, 2023.

Parker, Philip. *50 Things You Should Know about the Vikings (50 Things You Should Know About).* Beverly, MA: Quarto Publishing Group, 2022.

LEARN MORE ONLINE

1. Go to **www.factsurfer.com** or scan the QR code below.
2. Enter "**Tough Times Vikings** " into the search box.
3. Click on the cover of this book to see a list of websites.